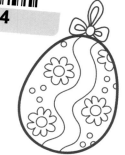

My EASTER Activity Book

Catherine Mackenzie
Puzzles and Illustrations
by Kim Shaw

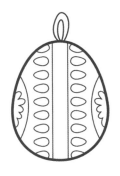

CF4·K

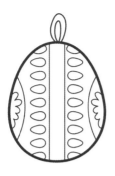

DEDICATION:

For my little friend – Fraser Mackenzie
CATHERINE

For my four wonderful grandchildren,
Zoe, Jack, Benjamin and Rebecca.
KIM

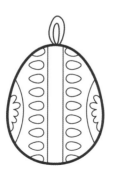

What's in this Book?

10 9 8 7 6 5 4 3 2
Copyright © 2016 Christian Focus Publications
Reprinted in 2023
ISBN:978-1-78191-913-2
Published by
Christian Focus Publications,
Geanies House, Fearn, Tain, Ross-shire, IV20 1TW, U.K.
Text by Catherine Mackenzie
Cover design by Daniel van Straaten
Illustrations by Kim Shaw
Printed and bound by Bell and Bain

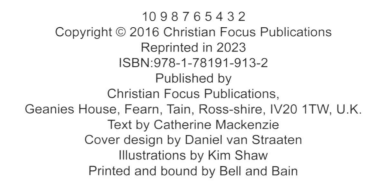

2 CORINTHIANS 8:9

For you know the grace of our Lord Jesus Christ, that though he was rich, yet for your sake he became poor, so that you by his poverty might become rich.

1. Mary Hears about Jesus

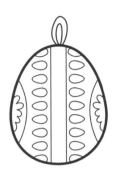

God sent an angel to the town of Nazareth in the land of Israel. This angel's name was Gabriel and he was sent to the home of a young Jewish girl called Mary. Gabriel told Mary that she was going to give birth to a baby boy and that she was to give him the name Jesus. The Lord God would give him the throne of David. But the throne and the kingdom were far greater than any human throne and kingdom. Jesus' Kingdom would never end.

Mary was engaged to a man called Joseph who was a descendant of King David. They weren't husband and wife yet so Mary was worried. 'How will this be?' she asked. 'I'm a virgin. I'm not married?' Gabriel told her that the Holy Spirit would come and God's power would overshadow her. 'The Holy one to be born will be called the Son of God.'

Look It Up:
Luke 1:26-38

2. Word Match

Match the crown shapes and write in the words in the correct order above.

7

3. Easter Promise

Jesus was born in Bethlehem. When he was eight days old, he was presented to God with a special ceremony. Every Jewish boy had to have this. Sometime later, Jesus was taken to the temple in Jerusalem. A man called Simeon saw the baby Jesus and knew immediately that this child was the promised Saviour of God. He took the child in his arms and praised God.

Mary and Joseph were amazed. Simeon told Mary that her baby boy would be spoken against and that a sword would pierce her soul. He was telling her what the future would bring. There would be great sadness in Mary's life.

Look It Up:
Luke 2:21-40

4. Puzzle it Out

Using the code to work out what Simeon said when he saw the Lord Jesus.

A	B	C	D	E	F	G	H	I	J	K	L	M
✿	◎	⊗	▷	✚	☾	•	◊	♡	৪	◇	☼	▢

N	O	P	Q	R	S	T	U	V	W	X	Y	Z
△	☺	↵	2	ව	৪	+	♈	✓	◉	⊠	∴	#

Simeon foretold how Jesus would bring the Good news of God's love to all people. Gentile is the name for people who are not Jewish. In the past, God told the Jewish people about himself. Now God was going to tell Jews and non-Jews about how God can forgive sin.

(coded message — Luke 2:29-32)

Luke 2:29-32

5. Jesus is Baptized

Look It Up: Matthew 3:13-17

Jesus grew up just like a normal boy, but he never sinned. This is because Jesus is God. He is sinless. Jesus became strong and was filled with wisdom. The grace of God was on him.

His cousin, John the Baptist, was preaching around the country. He told people to repent of their sin and to ask for forgiveness from God. Some people thought that John might be God's promised Saviour. But he told them that there was another one who would come, who was more powerful than he was. In fact, he was so great that John wasn't even good enough to untie his shoes.

When Jesus asked John to baptise him, John wasn't sure. 'I need to be baptized by you, and yet you come to me?' Jesus said, 'Let it be so now; it is proper for us to do this to fulfil all righteousness.'

John then baptized Jesus. As soon as Jesus came out of the water, heaven was opened and the Spirit of God came down from heaven like a dove and landed on Jesus.

6. Make it through the Maze

Find your way through the maze to the Bible verse.
When you are finished write the words
on the correct path through the
maze.

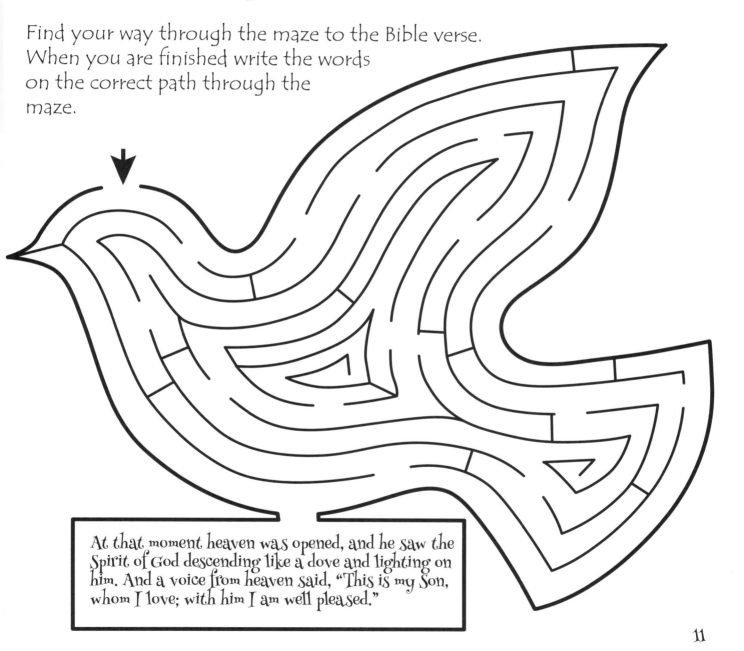

At that moment heaven was opened, and he saw the Spirit of God descending like a dove and lighting on him. And a voice from heaven said, "This is my Son, whom I love; with him I am well pleased."

7. Jesus is Tempted

Look It Up:
Matthew 4:1–11

After Jesus' baptism, he was led by the Holy Spirit into the desert. When he was there, he was tempted by the devil.

Jesus went without food for forty days and forty nights. He was hungry. The devil came to him and said 'If you are the Son of God, tell these stones to become bread.'

Jesus replied, 'It is written: "Man does not live on bread alone but on every word that comes from the mouth of God."'

The devil then took him to the highest point of the temple and told Jesus to throw himself off the top because God's Word says that angels would look after him. But Jesus told the devil that God's Word also says you should not put God to the test.

The devil then showed Jesus all the kingdoms of the world. 'I'll give it all to you if you will only bow down and worship me.' Jesus said to him, 'Get away from me Satan! For, it is written: "Worship the Lord your God, and serve him only."' The devil left him and angels came to help Jesus.

8. Object, Action, Result

Jesus performed miracles, but never because the devil said so. So that's why he didn't turn the stones into bread. In the list below there are things that we can change into other things. With a different colour of pen, draw a line between each object, each action and each result. One of these objects needs two actions before it gets its result and there are two miracles in the grid that only God can do. See if you can find these.

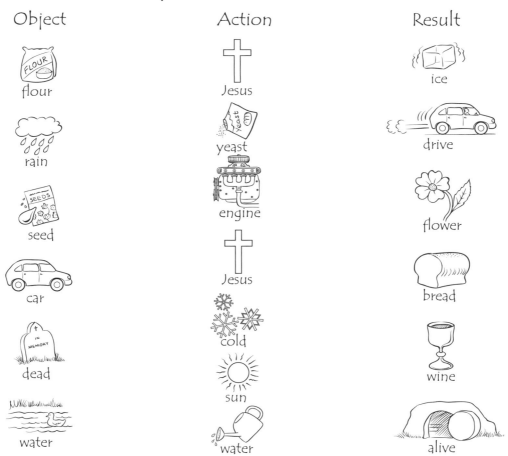

Object	Action	Result
flour	Jesus	ice
rain	yeast	drive
seed	engine	flower
car	Jesus	bread
dead	cold	wine
water	sun	alive
	water	

9. Jesus Teaches

Jesus taught a lot. He told people to obey God's Word. He also taught them how to pray to God and to trust in God. Jesus wanted people to be ready to meet with God. He knew that those who trusted in God would go to heaven and those who rejected God would go to hell. Jesus often taught people important lessons through stories that we call parables. One story was about a wise builder and a foolish builder. The wise builder took his time and built a house on a rock. It was a strong house. When the storm came, it stood firm. However, the foolish builder cut corners and built a house on the sand. It was easier and quicker to build, but when the storm came the whole house fell flat. The wise builder was ready for the storm. The foolish builder was not. Jesus wants people to listen to what God says and to obey him. When we obey God's Word we are like the wise builder – ready to face any problem because we trust in God.

Look It Up:
Luke 6:46-49

10. Find the Picture

Colour in each shape that has a dot. When you are finished you will have a silhouette of the Bible story.

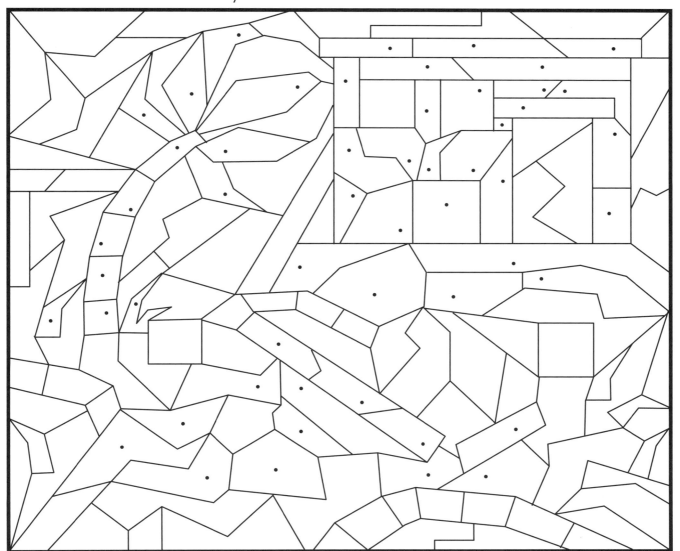

11. Jesus is Powerful

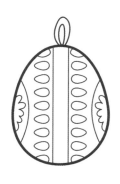

Jesus went back to his home town of Nazareth, but they did not like what he had to say and tried to kick him out of town. Some even tried to throw him off a cliff, but he walked right through the crowd and went on his way.

Look It Up:
Luke 4: 16–30.
Mark 1:21–28

When he was in Capernaum, he went to the synagogue. There he came across a man possessed by an evil spirit. The man cried out at the top of his voice, 'Ha! What do you want with us, Jesus of Nazareth? Have you come to destroy us? I know who you are – the Holy one of God!' 'Be quiet!' Jesus said sternly. 'Come out of him!' The demon then threw the man down and came out of him without injuring him. Everyone was amazed at the power and authority of Jesus!

12. Power Words

The Bible tells us how great God is. There is nothing and no one more powerful. Find the words in the verses below in the word search.

ROMANS 8:38–39

For I am **sure** that **neither death** nor **life**, nor **angels** nor **rulers**, nor things **present** nor things to **come**, nor **powers**, nor **height** nor **depth**, nor anything else in all **creation**, will be able to **separate** us from the **love** of **God** in **Christ Jesus** our **Lord**.

```
D  R  U  L  E  R  S  F  W  A  X
G  O  P  N  O  I  T  A  E  R  C
J  U  T  S  I  R  H  C  E  H  J
E  M  N  C  O  M  E  T  L  E  S
S  D  E  A  T  H  A  E  F  I  L
U  Q  I  Y  X  R  D  S  M  G  E
S  E  T  G  A  L  O  R  D  H  G
W  R  H  P  R  E  S  E  N  T  N
T  U  E  G  V  H  T  Z  V  I  A
I  S  R  A  O  S  R  E  W  O  P
O  H  T  P  E  D  N  G  L  N  L
```

13. Jesus Heals

Look It Up:
Mark 2:3-12

Jesus showed his power and authority by healing people. Jesus is God. He has amazing power. One day Jesus healed a man who couldn't walk. He could only lie flat on his bed. His friends wanted to take him to Jesus, but because of the huge crowds they couldn't get into the house that Jesus was in. So instead they carried their friend up to the roof and made a hole in it. They carefully lowered him on his bed down through the roof right in front of Jesus. Jesus said to the paralysed man, 'Friend your sins are forgiven.' The religious leaders were annoyed. They thought to themselves, 'Who can forgive sins, but God alone?'

Jesus knew what they were thinking and said, 'Why are you thinking these things? Which is easier to say, 'Your sins are forgiven,' or to say, 'Get up and walk? But so that you know that the Son of Man has authority on earth to forgive sins…' Jesus then turned to the paralysed man and said 'Take up your mat and go home.'

Immediately, he stood up, picked up his mat and went home praising God. Everyone was amazed.

14. Mat Man Maze

Help the friends find their way through the town to the house.

15. Peter Confesses

Look It Up:
Mark 8:27-53
Matthew 16:15-23

Jesus chose twelve men to be his disciples. They travelled with Jesus as he taught and preached and performed miracles. One day, after Jesus had been praying, he asked his disciples 'Who do the crowds say that I am?'

The disciples replied, 'Some say John the Baptist. Others say Elijah and still others, that one of the prophets from long ago has come back to life.'

Jesus asked another question, 'Who do you say that I am?' Simon Peter answered, 'You are the Christ, the Son of the living God.' Jesus replied, 'You are blessed, for this was not revealed to you by man but by my Father in heaven.'

From that time on, Jesus began to explain to his disciples that he must go to Jerusalem and suffer and be killed and on the third day raised to life. However, Peter argued with Jesus and said, 'This shall never happen to you.' Jesus rebuked him for Peter was saying what Satan wanted him to say, not what God wanted him to say.

16. Dig out the Disciples

Word search for all the disciples names.

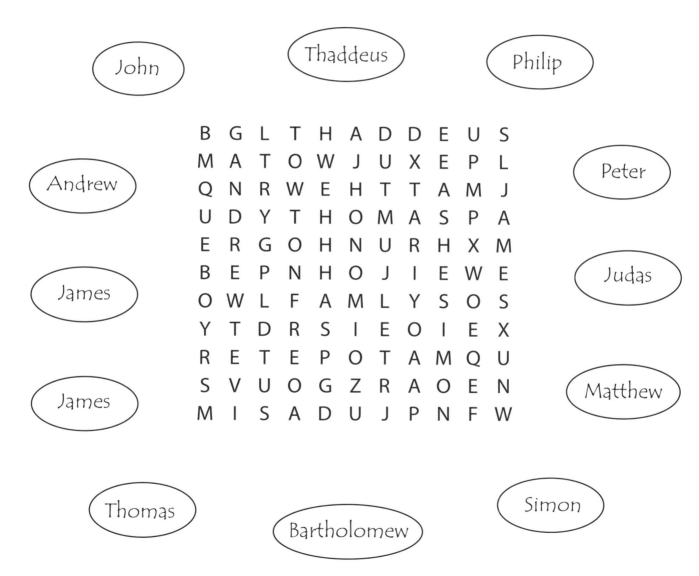

John

Thaddeus

Philip

Andrew

Peter

James

Judas

James

Matthew

Thomas

Simon

Bartholomew

```
B  G  L  T  H  A  D  D  E  U  S
M  A  T  O  W  J  U  X  E  P  L
Q  N  R  W  E  H  T  T  A  M  J
U  D  Y  T  H  O  M  A  S  P  A
E  R  G  O  H  N  U  R  H  X  M
B  E  P  N  H  O  J  I  E  W  E
O  W  L  F  A  M  L  Y  S  O  S
Y  T  D  R  S  I  E  O  I  E  X
R  E  T  E  P  O  T  A  M  Q  U
S  V  U  O  G  Z  R  A  O  E  N
M  I  S  A  D  U  J  P  N  F  W
```

17. The Mountain

One day, Jesus took Peter, John and James up a mountain to pray. As Jesus was praying, his face changed in its appearance and his clothes became as bright as lightning. Two men, Moses and Elijah, also appeared. They looked glorious and splendid and they were both talking with Jesus. Peter, James and John saw Jesus' glory and the two men with him. As the men were leaving, Peter said to Jesus, 'Master, it is good for us to be here. Let's put up three shelters one for you, one for Moses and one for Elijah.' Peter didn't know what he was saying. What he was saying was more than a bit silly. But while Peter was speaking, a cloud appeared and covered them and a voice came out of the cloud. It was God the Father who was speaking. When the voice stopped speaking, Peter, James and John discovered that they were alone with Jesus. To find out what God the Father said, do the next puzzle.

Look It Up:
Luke 9: 28-36

18. Find the Verse

Colour in the shapes with the dots to find the Bible verse.

19. Jesus Anointed

Jesus had many enemies, particularly the Jewish leaders. They were jealous of his power. 'If we let him go on everyone will believe in him,' they said. So they plotted to take his life.

Jesus withdrew to a quiet place where he stayed with his disciples. But six days before the Passover, Jesus arrived at Bethany. He went to stay with his friends Mary, Martha and their brother Lazarus. Lazarus was sitting with him at the table, and Martha was cooking the meal when Mary took a large bottle of expensive perfume and poured it on Jesus' feet.

One of Jesus' disciples, Judas, complained about the waste. It was worth a year's wages.

But Judas was a thief who would often help himself from the group's funds. Jesus told Judas to leave Mary alone. 'She saved this perfume for the day of my burial. You will always have the poor with you, but you will not always have me.' Jesus knew that the time was coming when he would be put to death.

Look It Up:
John 12:1-8

20. Sensational Scent

Make your own bottle of perfume. Take a plastic drinks bottle and fill it with scented tissues or pot pourri. Decorate the outside of the bottle with stickers and ribbons.

Photocopy and decorate this verse and stick it on the bottle somewhere.

Love the Lord your God with all your heart and with all your soul and with all your mind. Matthew 22:37

21. Jesus in Jerusalem

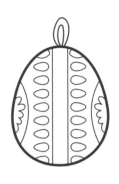

The day after his anointing, Jesus told his disciples to go and find a young donkey that had never been ridden. The disciples did this. Jesus rode the donkey into Jerusalem. A great crowd heard that Jesus was on his way. They took palm branches and went out to meet him shouting, 'Hosanna. Blessed is he who comes in the name of the Lord. Blessed is the king of Israel.' They also spread their coats on the road in front of him. As Jesus approached the city, he wept over it. He knew what was going to happen there in the future. He could see the great sin there. When Jesus entered the temple area, he saw that God's special house was being treated with disrespect. All the merchants wanted to do was make money for themselves and some people were charging too much. Jesus began to drive out the stall-holders and told them, 'God's house is a house of prayer, but you have made it a den of thieves.'

Extra Activity: Run your own lemonade stand and donate all the proceeds to charity.

Look It Up:
Matthew 21:1-13

22. Donkey Difference

Can you find the six differences between these two pictures?

23. The Lord's Supper

Look It Up:
Luke 22:14-23

Judas agreed to betray Jesus to the religious leaders for money. In the meantime, there was a special celebration called the Passover. Jesus wanted to celebrate this with his disciples, so he told them to get a room ready. When they were at the table, Jesus thanked God for the meal. He broke some bread and gave it to the disciples. Then he took some wine and gave it to them. In the future, when the disciples ate bread

and wine in this way, they remembered Jesus. But then something strange happened. Jesus said, 'The hand of the one who will betray me is with mine on the table. It is the one to whom I will give this piece of bread.' Jesus gave it to Judas. Judas immediately left the room.

Take the words in the bread and wine goblets and fit them into the blank spaces in the Bible verse below.

John 6:35 - Jesus said to them, 'I am the _ _ _ _ _ _ of _ _ _ _ ; whoever comes to me shall not _ _ _ _ _ _ _ , and whoever _ _ _ _ _ _ _ _ _ in me will never _ _ _ _ _ _ .'

24. Remember! Remember!

Jesus told his followers to eat the bread and drink the wine in order to remember him. Here is something you can make to remind you of God's goodness.

You will need:
Egg shells, egg box, cotton wool, pens, cress seeds.
It can take between 2 and 5 days for your cress seeds to grow.

Instructions:
1. Wash out some egg shells and sit them in the egg box.
2. Draw on some funny faces, use googly eyes if you have any.
3. Put cotton wool inside the shells and dampen this with some water.
4. Sprinkle cress seeds all over the cotton wool.
5. Put on a windowsill and wait for hair to sprout.
6. Add a little water to the cotton wool now and again.
7. Remember to write some words about God on the egg box.
8. Use the cress on your sandwiches when it is ready.
These bible verses will give you some ideas for words to write on your egg box: 1 John 4:8; 2 Chronicles 13:12; Psalm 18:2; 1 Corinthians 1:9

25. Peter's Boast

Peter was outspoken. He said things without thinking. He thought he was more important than he really was. One day, Peter said to Jesus that even if everyone else deserted him he wouldn't. This is what we call boasting. It's when we talk about ourselves and how great we are. It's being proud with our words. Peter was boasting that he was better than all the other disciples.

But Jesus knew what Peter was really like. God knows what is inside our hearts. There is nothing that is hidden from him. He knows the past and the future. Jesus told Peter that before the rooster crowed Peter would deny him three times. Peter didn't believe this. 'Even if I have to die with you I will never disown you.'

However, Jesus knew the truth about what was about to happen. It would be terrible. He had to pray to God, his Father, for help. So he took some of the disciples to the Mount of Olives to pray. He knew that God's plan was that he would be put to death. Jesus knew that he would be punished by God for the sins of others. Jesus prayed, 'Father, if you are willing take this cup from me; yet not my will, but yours be done.'

Look It Up:
Luke 22:31-34, 39-46

26. Story Wheel

You will need:
Two A4 sheets of thick card
or two paper plates.
Colouring pencils.
Scissors or a craft knife
A split pin fastener

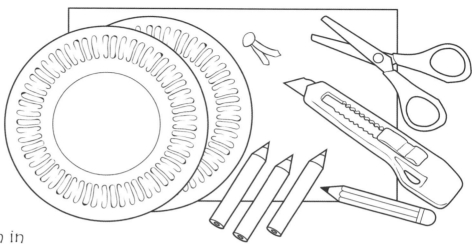

1. Cut two circles of card 20 cm in diameter or get two paper plates of that size.

2. Photocopy the story circle on the next page and colour the pictures. Stick it onto the centre of one circle or plate.

3. Copy or trace the circle on the following page and carefully cut out the window shape.

4. Push a split pin fastener through the centre of both circles or plates.

5. Spin the top circle to view the pictures and tell the story.

You could use this as a pattern to draw your own story wheel.

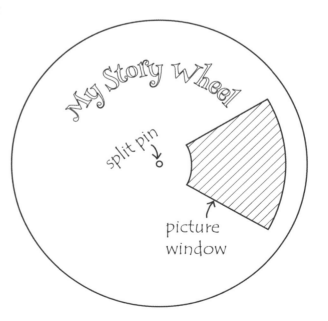

My Story Wheel

split pin

picture window

27. Jesus Prays

Look It Up:
John 17

Jesus spent a lot of time in prayer before he was arrested. He prayed for himself. 'Father the time has come. Glorify your Son, that your Son may glorify you.... I have brought you glory on earth by completing the work you gave me to do.'

Jesus also prayed for his disciples. 'All I have is yours, and all you have is mine. And glory has come to me through them. I will remain in the world no longer, but they are still in the world, and I am coming to you. Holy Father, protect them by the power of your name – the name you gave me – so that they may be one as we are one.'

He also prayed for all the believers who would come after them. 'Father, I want those you have given me to be with me where I am, and to see my glory, the glory you have given me because you loved me before the creation of the world.'

28. Prayer Box

Make your own prayer box: Write out things you want to thank God for, say sorry to God for, ask God for.

Find a small box with a lid – it can be cardboard, plastic or wooden. Maybe a chocolate box or a gift box, or a plastic container from the kitchen. The shape doesn't matter either – you could use a round cocoa tin.

Decorate your box with paint, pens or stickers. Photocopy the Prayer Box verse opposite and colour it in, then stick onto your box. Write your prayer requests on pieces of paper and keep them in your Prayer Box.

Prayer Box

"Do not be anxious about anything, but in every situation, by prayer and petition, with thanksgiving, present your requests to God."
Philippians 4:6

29. Jesus Betrayed

Look It Up:
John 18: 1–11, Luke 22:47–53

When Jesus finished praying, he left with his disciples and crossed the Kidron valley. On the other side there was an olive grove. However, Judas knew about this place as Jesus had often visited it with the disciples. Judas showed some soldiers and officials from the chief priests and pharisees where to go. Judas told the soldiers that the one he kissed was the one they had to arrest. Judas came up to Jesus to do this. The disciples asked Jesus if they should attack the soldiers. Peter didn't wait for a reply. He took out his sword and cut off a soldier's ear. Jesus said, 'Enough!' He touched the man's ear and healed it. At that point all the disciples deserted Jesus and fled.

30. Garden Grab

Jesus was arrested in the Garden of Gethsemane. Spot the six differences in the two pictures below.

31. Peter Denies Jesus

Look It Up:
Matthew 26: 57–75

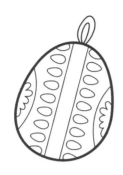

The soldiers who arrested Jesus took him to their commander, the High Priest, Caiaphas. Jesus was questioned by all the chief priests. They were looking for an excuse to kill him. Many people told lies about Jesus and when they asked Jesus, 'Are you the Christ, the Son of God?' Jesus replied, 'Yes.' 'He is worthy of death,' they exclaimed. They spat at Jesus and struck him with their fists.

Now Peter was sitting outside in the courtyard. Three times, people came up to him and asked if he was one of Jesus' disciples. Three times, Peter denied that he knew Jesus. Just then, a rooster crowed. Jesus turned and looked straight at Peter who remembered the words that Jesus had spoken earlier that day. 'Before the rooster crows, you will disown me three times.' Peter went outside and wept bitterly.

On the opposite page there is a picture for you to colour. Peter is weeping over his sin. Can you colour in the picture by working out what objects are either animal, mineral or vegetable? If it's animal use any colours you like. If the object is mineral, colour it in grey, brown, red or orange. If it is vegetable, colour it in green or yellow.

32. Peter Weeps

33. Jesus and Pilate

Look It Up:
Matthew 27: 11–31
Luke 22:63 – 23:25

Jesus suffered greatly before his crucifixion. He was beaten. He was mocked and insulted. The chief priests then sent him to Pilate, the Roman governor. But Pilate wasn't sure what to do with Jesus, so he sent him to King Herod. Herod eventually sent him back to Pilate. Jesus was made fun of again. They dressed him up in an elegant robe and twisted together a crown of thorns for his head. Then they called out in a mocking voice, 'Hail king of the Jews', and had him flogged. But Pilate couldn't find a reason to kill Jesus, so he asked the crowds of Jews who had gathered if he could release Jesus. The crowds called out again and again, 'Crucify him. Crucify him.' Finally Pilate agreed.

34. Pilate Puzzle: John 19:19–22

Break this code by using the first letter of each picture.

Pilate also wrote an inscription

and put it on the cross. It read, "Jesus of

Nazareth, the King of the Jews." Many of the Jews

read this inscription, for the place where Jesus was

crucified was near the city, and it was

written in Aramaic, in Latin and in

Greek. So the chief priests of the Jews said to Pilate,

"Do not write 'The King of the Jews,' but rather, 'This

man said, I am King of the Jews." Pilate answered,

'What I have written I have written."

35. The Crucifixion

Look It Up:
Matthew 27: 32–56

As they led Jesus away, they grabbed hold of a man from the crowd called Simon from Cyrene. Simon was made to carry the cross for Jesus as he made his way to Golgotha, a terrible place where criminals were put to death. Jesus was not a criminal. He wasn't even a sinner. On either side of Jesus a criminal was also nailed to a cross. One was angry at Jesus, the other asked Jesus to forgive him. Jesus said to the one who asked for forgiveness, 'Today you will be with me in paradise.' When he died, Jesus said to God, 'Father, into your hands I commit my spirit.' A Roman centurion, who saw all that went on, was astonished. 'Surely this was the Son of God.'

36. Jesus' Words Jigsaw

Here are some other words that Jesus said when he was on the cross. Join them up.

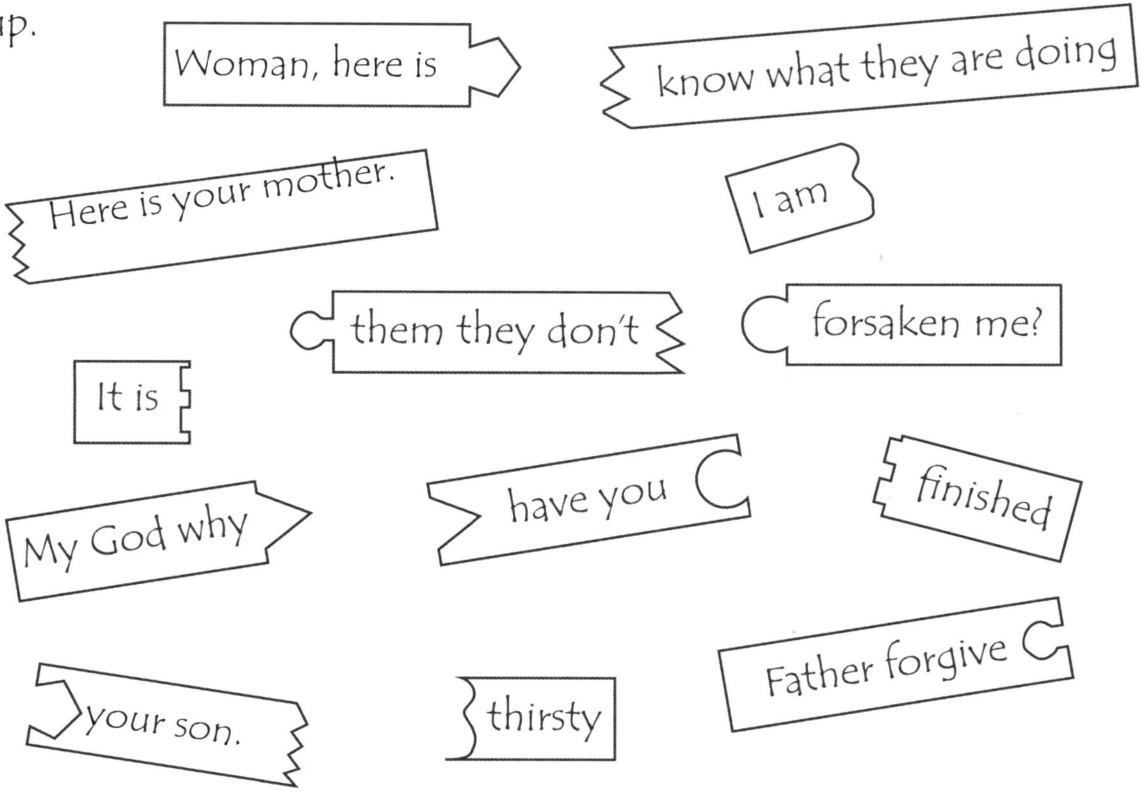

Woman, here is

know what they are doing

Here is your mother.

I am

them they don't

forsaken me?

It is

My God why

have you

finished

your son.

thirsty

Father forgive

37. Jesus is Buried

When Jesus had died, two men, Joseph and Nicodemus, came to Pilate and asked him if they could take Jesus' body away to be buried. He said 'Yes,' and Jesus' body was taken down from the cross and buried in a brand new tomb. Some women who had been friends of Jesus came and saw where his body was buried. They went home to get things ready. After they had rested on God's special day they came back to the tomb to anoint Jesus' body with spices and perfumes.

Look It Up:
Matthew 27: 57–66
John 19:38–42

38. Wonderful Words

This verse from Isaiah was written hundreds of years before Jesus was even born – yet it speaks of exactly what happened to the Lord Jesus after his death. See if you can crack the code.

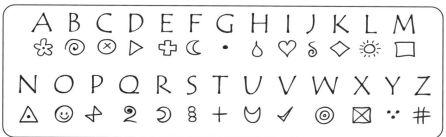

A B C D E F G H I J K L M
N O P Q R S T U V W X Y Z

ISAIAH 53:9

(coded message on scroll)

39. Back to life

When the women arrived early at the tomb, they found that the stone had been rolled away and there was no body there! What a puzzle! Suddenly, two men in gleaming clothes stood beside them. The women were frightened, but the men asked, 'Why are you looking for the living amongst the dead? He is not here, he has risen. Remember how he told you that on the third day he would rise again.'

Look It Up:
Luke 24: 1–12
John 20: 1–9

The women rushed back to tell the disciples about what they had just discovered. Peter didn't believe the news and had to go and check it out for himself. He rushed to the tomb and went in, only to find it empty with the strips of linen lying by themselves. The cloth that had been around Jesus' head was folded by itself separate from the linen. Peter wasn't sure what had happened.

40. Peter's Puzzle

Help Peter find his way through the maze to the empty tomb.

41. And there's More

Jesus Appears to the Disciples

Not long after, Jesus appeared to the disciples when they were in a locked room.
They thought he was a ghost. But Jesus said, 'Look at my hands and feet. A ghost does not have flesh and bones. Peace be with you. As the Father has sent

Look It Up:
John 20:19-23;
Mark 16:15-19

me so I am sending you.' Then he breathed on them and said, 'Receive the Holy Spirit.'

   Jesus told the disciples to 'Go into all the world and preach the good news.' He was then taken up to heaven. Now he is at God's right hand. He will one day return as a victorious king. If you trust in Jesus and have asked God to forgive you for your sins – you will be saved, receive eternal life, and be part of the victory.

Work out the following Bible verse by using the code.

A B C D E F G H I J K L M

N O P Q R S T U V W X Y Z

Bible Readings

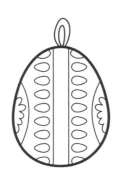

Day 1 –2 Luke 1:26–38

Day 3–4 Luke 2:21–40

Day 5–6 Matthew 3:13–17

Day 7–8 Matthew 4:1–11

Day 9–10 Luke 6:46–49

Day 11–12 Luke 4: 16–30.

Mark 1:21–28

Day 13–14 Mark 2:3–12

Day 15–16 Mark 8:27–33, Matthew 16:15–23

Day 17–18 Luke 9: 28–36

Day 19–20 John 12:1–8

Day 21–22 Matthew 21:1–13

Day 23–24 Luke 22:14–23

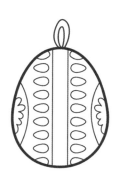

Day 25–26 Luke 22:31–34, 39–46

Day 27–28 John 17

Day 29–30 John 18: 1–11,

Luke 22:47–53

Day 31–32 Matthew 26: 57–75

Day 33–34 Matthew 27: 11–31,

Luke 22:63 – 23:25

Day 35–36 Matthew 27: 32–56

Day 37–38 Matthew 27: 57–66,

John 19:38–42

Day 39–40 Luke 24: 1–12,

John 20:1–9

Day 41 John 20:19–23,

Mark 16:15–19

Answers

Day 2.: Word Match

He will be great and will be called the Son of the Most High.

Day 4.: Puzzle it Out

Sovereign, Lord as you have promised, you now dismiss your servant in peace. For my eyes have seen your salvation, which you have prepared in the sight of all people, a light for revelation to the Gentiles and for glory to your people Israel.

Day 6

Day 12

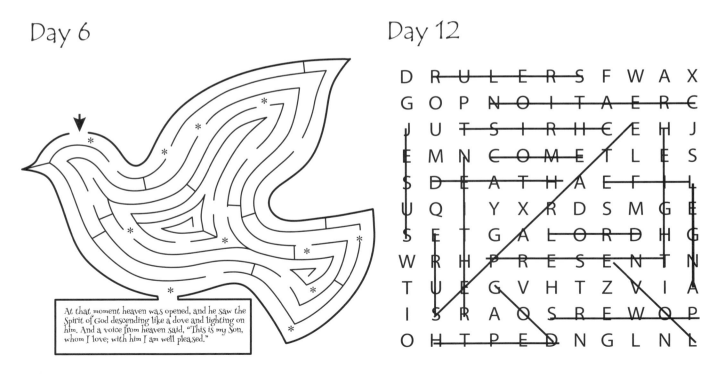

At that moment heaven was opened, and he saw the Spirit of God descending like a dove and lighting on him. And a voice from heaven said, "This is my Son, whom I love; with him I am well pleased."

Day 8.: Object, Action, Result
Flour + Yeast = Bread
Seed + Water+ Sun = Flower
Dead + Jesus = Alive

Rain + Cold = Ice
Car + Engine = Drive
Water + Jesus = Wine

Day 14: Mat Man Maze
The little stars will show you the way in and out of the maze.

Day 14

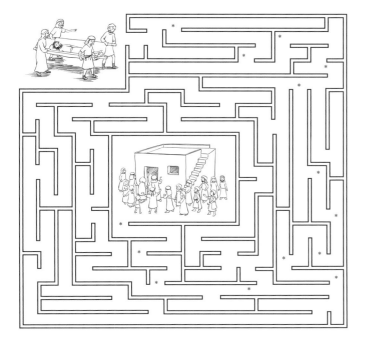

Day 16

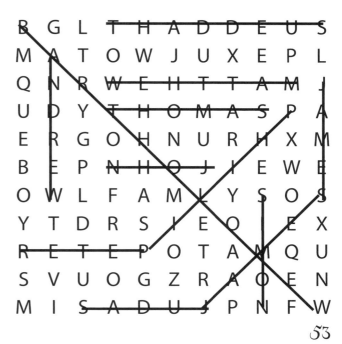

Day 18: Find the Verse

This is my Son whom I have chosen, listen to him. Luke 9:35

Day 22: Donkey Difference

Six differences. Picture 2 has... 1. A donkey blanket. 2. One vase at the bottom of the steps. 3. A tree on the hill. 4. A window on the wall. 5. An arch shaped door. 6. No man at the top of the steps.

Day 23. The Lord's Supper

Jesus said to them, 'I am the bread of life; whoever comes to me shall not hunger, and whoever believes in me will never thirst.'

Day 30: Garden Grab

Six differences. The first picture has: 1. Judas in a striped coat 2. Four torches 3. Soldier 3 has a sword in his hand 4. Less plants on the left rock 5. A missing tree on the far right 6. A missing flower on the bush.

Day 34: Pilate Puzzle

Pilate, inscription, cross, Jesus, Jews, crucified, city, Aramaic, Latin, Greek, king, written. The object pictures are: Pig, Ice cream, Lamp, Apple, Tree, Egg, Nest, Snake, Cat, Rainbow, Owl, Jelly, Umbrella, Wellington Boot, Fish, Door, Yoyo, Mouse, Giraffe, Knife.

Day 36: Jesus' Words Jigsaw

Woman behold your son. Behold your mother; It is Finished; I am Thirsty; My God why have you forsaken me; Father forgive them, they don't know what they are doing. (Look up John 19:26-27; John 19:30; John 19:28; Mark 15:34; Luke 23:34)

Day 38: Wonderful Words

And they made his grave with the wicked and with a rich man in his death, although he had done no violence, and there was no deceit in his mouth.

Day 40: Peter's Puzzle
Join up the stars to work out the correct way in and out of the maze.

41: And there's More
Thanks be to God who gives us the victory through our Lord Jesus Christ.

Jesus' Birth:
Luke 2: 10-11

The angel said to them, 'Fear not, for behold, I bring you good news of great joy that will be for all the people. For unto you is born this day in the city of David a Saviour, who is Christ the Lord.'

Jesus' Life:
Mark 1:14-15

Now after John was arrested, Jesus came into Galilee, proclaiming the gospel of God, and saying, 'The time is fulfilled, and the kingdom of God is at hand; repent and believe the good news.'

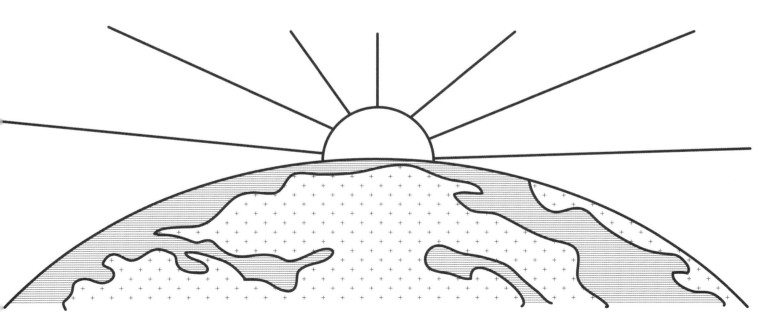

Jesus' Death:
Romans 5:6-8

For while we were still weak, at the right time Christ died for the ungodly. For one will scarcely die for a righteous person—though perhaps for a good person one would dare even to die—but God shows his love for us in that while we were still sinners, Christ died for us.

Jesus' Resurrection:
1 Peter 1:3

Blessed be the God and Father of our Lord Jesus Christ! According to his great mercy, he has caused us to be born again to a living hope through the resurrection of Jesus Christ from the dead.

Jesus' Ascension:
Luke 24: 51-52

While he blessed them, he parted from them and was carried up into heaven. And they worshipped him and returned to Jerusalem with great joy.

Jesus' Return:
Acts 1:11

This Jesus, who was taken up from you into heaven, will come in the same way you as you saw him go into heaven.

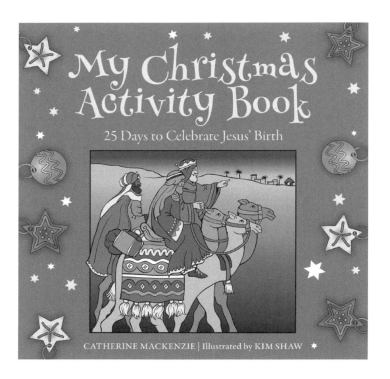

It's the countdown to Christmas. There are 25 days to go until we celebrate the birth of Jesus Christ, the Son of God. In this book there are puzzles and codes, activities and crafts to help you remember the real reason for Christmas – the fact that God sent his Son to the world so that people could become God's friends once more.

Look out for the full colour pull out advent calendar! Something you can use each day as you go through the book and as you count the days until the big day itself.

ISBN: 978-1-78191-759-6

The experiences and beliefs we want our children to have don't just happen!
It's hard work. They demand our time and energy. God's command is that
his commandments are to be on our hearts and we are to 'impress them on
our children'. So this book is a starting point with simple and easy to prepare
ways for you to guide and encourage your children in the faith and hope-
fully have fun while you are at it.

- 82 devotional life lessons and simple prayers
- Spend time together and talk about the important things in life
- Special Features: Bible Reading, Play, Say, Pray, Memory Verse

ISBN: 9-78178191-589-9

Christian Focus Publications

Christian Focus Publications publishes books for adults and children under its four main imprints: Christian Focus, CF4K, Mentor and Christian Heritage. Our books reflect our conviction that God's Word is reliable and Jesus is the way to know him, and live for ever with him.

Our children's publication list covers pre-school to early teens. We also publish personal and family devotional titles, biographies and inspirational stories that children will love.

From pre-school board books to teenage apologetics, we have it covered!

CF4•K
Because you're never
too young to know Jesus

CHRISTIAN FOCUS PUBLICATIONS

Christian Focus | Christian Heritage | CF4K | Mentor